COBBLESTONE · THE CIVIL WAR

Abraham Lincoln
Defender of the Union

Cobblestone Publishing
A Division of Carus Publishing
Peterborough, NH
www.cobblestonepub.com

Staff

Editorial Director: Lou Waryncia
Editor: Sarah Elder Hale
Book Design: David Nelson, www.dnelsondesign.com
Proofreaders: Meg Chorlian, Eileen Terrill

Text Credits

The content of this volume is derived from articles that first appeared in *COBBLESTONE* and *APPLESEEDS* magazines.
Contributors: Craig E. Blohm, Louise Classon, Mary Morton Cowan, Karan Davis Cutler, Henry Dubroff, Karen H. Dusek, Camille Floyd, Sarah Elder Hale, Ellen Hardsog, Harold Holzer, Ruth Tenzer Feldman, Carolyn Johnson, Carolyn Liberatore Lavine, Edison McIntyre, Christina Mierau, Ann Woodbury Moore, George L. Painter, Laurel Sherman, Linda Norbut Suits

Picture Credits

National Museum of American History: 3; Clipart.com: 4, 6, 7, 8, 11, 12 (top), 13, 17, 19, 23, 24, 26, 28, 29, 30, 31, 33, 35, 36, 37, 38, 40, 41, 42 (left), 43; Library of Congress: 5, 9, 10, 12 (bottom), 15, 16, 22, 27, 32, 33 (inset), 34, 39, 42 (right); Photos.com: 18; Fred Carlson: 20–21. Images for "Civil War Time Line," pages 44–45, courtesy of Photos.com, Clipart.com, and Library of Congress.

Cover

Dennis Malone Carter, *Lincoln Enters Richmond*
Courtesy of the Chicago Historical Society.

Library of Congress Cataloging-in-Publication Data

Abraham Lincoln : defender of the Union / [project director, Lou Waryncia; editor, Sarah Elder Hale].

p. cm. -- (Cobblestone the Civil War)

Includes index.

ISBN 0-8126-7902-4 (hardcover)

Lincoln, Abraham, 1809-1865—Juvenile literature. 2. Presidents—United States--Biography--Juvenile literature. 3. United States--History--Civil War, 1861-1865--Juvenile literature. 4. United States--Politics and government --1861-1865--Juvenile literature. 5. United States--Politics and government --1849-1861--Juvenile literature.

I. Waryncia, Lou. II. Hale, Sarah Elder. III. Series.

E457.905.A295 2005

973.7'092--dc22

[B]

2005015214

Printed in China

Cobblestone Publishing

30 Grove Street, Suite C
Peterborough, NH 03458
www.cobblestonepub.com

Table of Contents

From Log House to State House

Abe Lincoln was born in this small log cabin in Kentucky. When he was 7 years old his family moved farther west to Indiana.

Abraham Lincoln's rise to the presidency did not come easily. In fact, young Abe worked hard and dealt with struggles throughout his childhood. His early political career saw more failure than success. He lost his first election, finishing eighth among 13 candidates. Lincoln had known setbacks before, and he would have others, but he possessed a determination to succeed that was born in the rugged country where he grew up.

Childhood on the Frontier

In 1806, Thomas Lincoln married Nancy Hanks. The couple settled near Elizabethtown, Kentucky, where their daughter, Sarah, was born in 1807.

The Lincolns owned a series of farms, but Thomas grew barely enough food to feed his family. He made most of his living as a

Tall, Tough, and Fast

Young Abe was taller and tougher than most boys his age. At 14, he was six feet tall, an extraordinary size for boys at the time. He was muscular, too, from all the physical work he had done throughout his childhood. When he wasn't working, he enjoyed testing his strength as an athlete — his favorite sports were wrestling and running.

skilled carpenter. He built the one-room log cabin near Hodgenville where Abraham was born on February 12, 1809.

In later years, Abe remembered little about Kentucky. He was just seven years old when his family decided to leave Kentucky and move farther west, across the Ohio River to Indiana. The Lincolns settled in what is now Spencer County, a few miles north of the river. Although Indiana became a state that year, 1816, the land

When he finished with his chores on the family farm, young Abe Lincoln hired himself out for jobs such as splitting logs for rail fences.

along the Ohio was dense forest, with few trails or settlements. Abe and his family spent their first Indiana winter in a rough lean-to shelter while Thomas built a cabin.

Hard Work, Tough Lessons

Around the time of Abe's eighth birthday, the Lincolns moved into their new home. Abe was tall and strong for his age. He took up an ax to cut down the surrounding trees and hitched up a team to plow the fields he had cleared. He hauled water to the new house from the nearest spring, a mile away.

The farm began to yield good crops, and as more settlers came to the area, Thomas found more work as a carpenter. But 1818 was a cruel year. A disease called milk-sick struck the community. It killed Nancy, who was then just 34 years old.

About a year after Nancy died, Thomas went back to Elizabethtown. When he returned to Indiana, he brought with him a new wife. Sarah Bush Johnston Lincoln, a widow with three children, was warm and loving; she quickly adopted Abe and Sarah as her own.

Rail-Splitter and Ferryman

By age 14, Abe was old enough to work away from the Lincoln farm when his father could spare him. Over the next few years, he had several jobs — clearing land, splitting logs for fence rails, helping to run a ferry — and he gave most of his earnings to his father. When he was 19, he helped guide a flatboat loaded with produce down the Mississippi River to

Dealing With Death

Frontier life taught some hard lessons, the greatest being the loss of loved ones at an early age. Abe's younger brother, Thomas, died when only a baby; his sister, Sarah, died at age 20 while bearing her first child. When Abe was 10, he nearly died after being kicked by a horse.

New Orleans. It was his first trip to a big city.

In 1830, the Lincoln family moved west again, this time to Illinois. Soon afterward, Abe left home and began working in a general store in New Salem, a small settlement near Springfield. He enjoyed roughhousing with his new friends and loved to wrestle, but he also spent many hours reading. He joined a debating group and, in 1831, voted for the first time.

The Pull of Politics

The following year, Lincoln decided to run for the Illinois legislature. His campaign was severely delayed when he volunteered to serve in the Black Hawk War. He returned to New Salem in late July and campaigned hard, but he lost the election. Still, Lincoln got 277 of the 300 votes in his hometown, and that encouraged him to run again. In 1834, with overwhelming support from New Salem, Lincoln won a seat in the legislature. It was just the beginning for the frontier boy who would eventually be one of our most famous presidents.

Respect for Learning

As a young boy, Abe learned to value knowledge. His parents, Thomas and Nancy, had little formal education. In fact, Thomas could hardly sign his name, while Nancy signed with an X. Still, they had great respect for learning. Nancy loved to tell Bible stories to Sarah and Abe, and before the family left Kentucky, she sent Abe to a small school near their home.

Like his mother, Abe's stepmother, Sarah Bush Johnston Lincoln, encouraged him to learn all he could. Over several years, Abe received fewer than 12 months of schooling, but at age 12 he could read, write, and do a bit of arithmetic. An eager student, Abe often walked several miles to borrow books. He read the Bible, *Aesop's Fables*, *Robinson Crusoe*, *Pilgrim's Progress*, *The Arabian Nights*, a biography of George Washington — anything he could find. According to Abe's cousin Dennis Hanks, "I never saw Abe after he was 12 that he didn't have a book in his hand or in his pocket. It didn't seem natural to see a feller read like that." He enjoyed listening to his father and other adults talk late into the night about farming, politics, and life.

Years later, as a candidate for state office, Lincoln spoke in support of free schools, saying that education was "the most important subject which we as a people can be engaged in."

Mary Todd Lincoln

On the evening of November 4, 1842, in the parlor of her sister's home, Mary Todd married Abraham Lincoln. Although her family objected to this match with the rugged and penniless lawyer born on the frontier, Mary said, "I would rather marry a good man — a man of mind — with a hope and bright prospects ahead for position — fame & power than to marry all the houses — gold…in the world."

From their first meeting in 1839, at a ball in Springfield, Illinois, the differences between Todd and Lincoln would be glaring. He was tall and lean and had been born in a log cabin. She was short and plump, with a more refined upbringing. But their relationship was one of genuine love.

History has not always been kind to Mary Todd Lincoln. She was a complicated and often misunderstood woman, and she remains so today. Too often she is remembered for her fights, wild spending, and later insanity. What is not mentioned is her intelligence, kindness, and immense love for her husband and family.

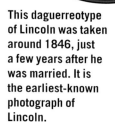

This daguerreotype of Lincoln was taken around 1846, just a few years after he was married. It is the earliest-known photograph of Lincoln.

Miss Todd

Mary Ann Todd was born on December 13, 1818, to wealthy parents in Lexington, Kentucky. She was the fourth of seven children. Her mother died when she was six, and less than 18 months later, her father married Elizabeth Humphreys. Mary did not get along with her stepmother, who had nine more children. She became lost in the crowd and later described her childhood as "desolate."

Mary was a good student, and her escape from her situation was boarding school. Because she did not get along with her stepmother, she soon considered Madame Mentelle's school her home. In all, Mary attended school for 10 years, much longer than most girls at the time, who usually received only enough education to make them good wives and mothers.

A Suitable Match?

In 1837, Mary spent three months in Springfield, Illinois, visiting her older sister Elizabeth Todd Edwards. Elizabeth and her husband were prominent in Springfield society, and Mary enjoyed her visit. She returned to Springfield to stay in 1839, and it was then that she met and married Lincoln.

The Todd family opposed the match because Lincoln did not fit their idea of a suitable husband. He was not wealthy and did not travel in the same social circles as the Todds. Mary's sister also felt that they were incompatible in "natures, mind — education — raising &c."

But Mary believed that she and Abraham had much in common. Both had lost their mothers at an early age. Both were intelligent and loved to read. And, most important, both liked to discuss politics.

Mary was known to have a sharp tongue, and the Lincolns, like many couples, argued. The cause of many of their

Mary Todd Lincoln received a formal education and possessed social graces that her husband lacked. Despite their differences, Mary and Abraham cared deeply for each other and shared a passion for politics.

disagreements was Lincoln's long absences, sometimes up to six months, while he was a lawyer on the Eighth Circuit. They also quarreled about his lack of refined manners. Yet their marriage was strong and built on mutual affection. While a congressman in Washington, D.C., Lincoln wrote, "When you were here, I thought you hindered me some in attending to business; but now, having nothing but business — no variety — it has grown exceedingly tasteless to me…. I hate to stay in this old room by myself."

Several Union generals and other dignitaries attended the second inaugural reception at the White House. The President (center) is shown greeting Mrs. Ulysses S. Grant as Mary Todd Lincoln (in pink) looks on.

Caught in the Middle

Mary's greatest difficulties began after the Lincoln family moved into the White House. Many Northerners saw her as a traitor because she was from the South. Conversely, many of her siblings sided with the Confederates, who saw her as a traitor because she was married to the despised president of the Union.

Despite her education and grace, easterners saw her as an uncouth westerner. The newspapers usually wrote only about her fine clothes and extravagant spending and not about her visits to hospitals and other charitable activities.

Because of the war and his other presidential duties, Lincoln spent little time with Mary. She wrote, "I consider myself fortunate, if at eleven o'clock, I once more find myself, in my pleasant room and very especially, if my tired and weary Husband is there…."

Faced With Tragedy

Mary also had much tragedy in her life. While still in Springfield in 1850, the Lincolns' second son, Eddie, died shortly before his fourth birthday. Twelve years later, in the White House, their third son, Willie, died when he was 11. Willie's death affected Mary deeply. She even tried to contact his spirit and said that he came to the foot of her bed at night. The final blow was her husband's assassination while he was sitting next to her at Ford's Theatre.

After Lincoln's death, Mary traveled all over the United States and Europe with her youngest son, Tad, trying to find peace. Sadly, Tad died in 1871 after a long illness, and Mary's mental state continued to deteriorate. Eventually, her lone remaining son, Robert, began court proceedings to judge her sanity. She was found insane and spent nearly four months in a mental hospital.

After her release and more travel, she returned to Springfield in 1880 and spent her remaining days with her sister Elizabeth. Ironically, she lived in the very house where Lincoln had given her the wedding ring engraved "Love Is Eternal." She died on July 16, 1882.

The Lincolns' Springfield, Illinois, home is located on the corner of Eighth and Jackson streets. They lived here for 17 years — until 1861, when they moved to the White House in Washington, D.C.

11

Lincoln's Sons

Although the Lincolns had four sons, only their oldest child, Robert, lived to adulthood. Eddie, the Lincolns' second son, did not even live past the age of four. He died in February 1850 of consumption, a disease of the lungs. Their third son, Willie, was 11 when he died in 1862 after a long illness.

Willie and Tad

Willie and his younger brother, Tad, enjoyed the distinction of being the first presidential children to live in the White House. Tad (few people called him by his given name, Thomas) was the youngest Lincoln son, born on April 4, 1853. He was a month shy of his eighth birthday when his father was inaugurated. When he and 10-year-old Willie were shown around their new home, their mother wrote that they eagerly "interviewed" all the servants, sizing up the possibilities for the fun they could have in the mansion.

Though a trial for the staff, the young boys' presence in the White House was a delight for their father. The boys loved playing jokes on others. Once, while

Lincoln adored his sons and spent as much time with them as his busy public life allowed. Willie (above) and Tad (right, with his father) were the first presidential children to live in the White House.

experimenting with the White House bells, they made all the bells ring, summoning all of Lincoln's secretaries.

Willie's death in the winter of 1862 was a severe blow to the family. Tad's prankish nature, however, continued to amuse his father, and with Robert at college, Tad became the immediate focus of all his parents' love. Consequently, he ran wild and studied little. After his father's assassination, Tad lived with his mother in Chicago and later in Europe before he died after a long illness in 1871, at the age of 18.

Robert Todd Lincoln

Lincoln's sole surviving son, Robert Todd Lincoln, was born on August 1, 1843, and he lived to be 83 years old. He graduated from Harvard in 1864 and enlisted in the Union army in February 1865, joining General Ulysses S. Grant's staff as a captain. After his father's death, he moved to Chicago, where he became a prominent lawyer and businessman.

Although Robert served as secretary of war from 1881 to 1885 and as minister (ambassador) to Great Britain from 1889 to 1893, he repeatedly refused to enter politics, saying, "I have seen enough of the inside of Washington official life to have lost all interest in it." Oddly, he was nearby at the assassinations of three U.S. presidents — his father in 1865, James A. Garfield in 1881, and William McKinley in 1901. Once, when asked if he would attend an official function, Robert reportedly replied, "No, I'm not going and they'd better not invite me, because there is a certain fatality about [them] when I am present."

Although critics accused him of being pompous and aloof, Robert's friends found him loyal, kind, generous, and — like his father — an excellent storyteller.

The eldest of the Lincoln children, Robert, attended Harvard University and served in the Civil War under General Ulysses S. Grant.

A Stand Against Slavery

During the early 1850s, Abraham Lincoln devoted most of his attention to his law practice, which was growing into one of the largest in the state of Illinois. In 1854, he once again became active in the political arena. This occurred after congressional passage of the Kansas–Nebraska Act, which Senator Stephen A. Douglas of Illinois had spearheaded through Congress.

Slowing the Spread of Slavery

The Kansas–Nebraska Act established the territories of Kansas and Nebraska, which had previously been referred to simply as Kansas. The organization of this vast region had been delayed by controversy between the North and the South over the question of whether slavery would be allowed to spread into territories where it was not already established.

In Congress, four previous attempts to organize a single territory had been unsuccessful, chiefly because of slaveholding states' opposition to the Missouri Compromise. Enacted by Congress more than 30 years earlier, the Missouri Compromise had become a time-honored barrier to the extension of slavery. Under its terms, Missouri had been allowed to enter the Union as a slave state, and territories from the Louisiana Purchase that were south of latitude 36°30' were permitted to have slavery. The institution was prohibited north of that line, including the area known as Kansas.

Letting the States Decide

Because the West was being settled rapidly, Douglas regarded the territorial organization of Kansas as an urgent matter. In an attempt to win over slaveholding states, he introduced legislation that left the question of slavery up to the territorial settlers.

A slave is offered for sale at a Southern slave market. In the mid-1800s, most slaves were American born, descendants of slaves brought from Africa in the 18th century.

Politicians of the day, including Lincoln (far left) and Douglas (second from left), fought over the issue of slavery, especially in new states. Lincoln was afraid that the Kansas–Nebraska Act would allow slavery to spread to western states.

Douglas called this the principle of "popular sovereignty."

This feature of the Kansas–Nebraska Act contradicted the provisions of the Missouri Compromise, but an amendment to the original version of the bill explicitly repealed the 1820 legislation. The Kansas–Nebraska Act was signed into law on May 30, 1854.

Douglas saw the settlement of the West as essential and regarded slavery as a less important issue, although he expressed the hope that Kansas and Nebraska would remain free. Lincoln took a very different view of the Kansas–Nebraska Act. The legislation alarmed him because it allowed the introduction of slavery into territory where the Missouri Compromise had prohibited it for more than three decades.

Lincoln Says 'No'

Although Lincoln had taken stands opposing slavery in his earlier service in the Illinois House of Representatives and U.S. Congress, prior to 1854 he did not regard it as a momentous national issue. He later explained that he held this view because he believed that the institution would eventually disappear. The Kansas–Nebraska Act shattered Lincoln's hope. From 1854 on, slavery became a focus of his public statements on political issues.

After the act was passed and Congress went into recess, an outraged public made their feelings known. Senator Douglas noted that on a journey from Washington to Illinois, "all along the Western Reserve of Ohio I could find my effigy upon every tree we passed." Douglas then embarked on a speaking tour throughout Illinois to support Democratic candidates for Congress and the state legislature. In his speeches, he also defended the legislation with which he was now identified.

In September 1854, Lincoln again became a candidate for the Illinois House of Representatives. Although he was not running directly against Douglas, the Kansas–Nebraska Act was the major point of contention in the 1854 campaign. The political debates

The Missouri Compromise, 1820

As cotton became a bigger and bigger crop and Americans pushed westward, slavery spread into new states, including Alabama and Mississippi. When the lands that had been bought in the Louisiana Purchase of 1803 began to come up for statehood, a new conflict arose. The North wanted to stop the spread of slavery, while the South wanted to allow slavery. Henry Clay, a congressman from Kentucky, submitted legislation to deal with the growing political divide. The agreement finally reached in 1820 was called the Missouri Compromise. Under the Compromise, the new state of Missouri would enter the Union as a slave state, while Maine, which was not yet a state, would enter as a free state. This meant that there would be a total of 12 free and 12 slave states in the country. The Compromise also stated that slavery would not be allowed in any new states north of Missouri's southern border, or the 36° 30' line of latitude.

An Excerpt from Lincoln's Peoria Speech

"**S**lavery is founded in the selfishness of man's nature — opposition to it is [in] his love of justice. These principles are an eternal antagonism; and when brought into collision so fiercely, as slavery extension brings them, shocks, and throes, and convulsions must ceaselessly follow. Repeal the Missouri Compromise — repeal all compromises — repeal the Declaration of Independence — repeal all past history, you still cannot repeal human nature. It still will be [in] the abundance of man's heart, that slavery extension is wrong; and out of the abundance of his heart, his mouth will continue to speak."

between Lincoln and Douglas in 1854 (and later in 1858) galvanized Lincoln's position on slavery.

The Peoria Speech

As part of the debates, Lincoln delivered a major three-hour speech at Peoria on the evening of October 16, 1854. Although a self-contained statement, it was intended to answer a speech given earlier in the day by Douglas. Some historians have called Lincoln's Peoria speech his first great address.

In Peoria, Lincoln attacked Douglas's Kansas–Nebraska Act. He said, "I think, and shall try to show, that it is wrong; wrong in its direct effect, letting slavery into Kansas and Nebraska — and wrong in its prospective principle, allowing it to spread to every other part of the wide world, where men can be found inclined to take it."

The Peoria speech was the most open and forceful statement on the immorality of

Unshackled!

Since 1619, when 20 enslaved Africans were brought to the Virginia colony, slavery had been a divisive political issue in America. Lincoln fought vigorously to halt its spread and ultimately abolish the institution.

slavery that Lincoln had made, and this stand would remain an important part of his future discussions of the issue. The speech included another theme that would continue to be a significant element of Lincoln's political statements: preservation of the Union. Lincoln called upon his fellow citizens to limit the spread of slavery by returning to the principles of the nation's founders: "If we do this, we shall not only have saved the Union; but we shall have so saved it, as to make, and to keep it, forever worthy of the saving."

After Peoria, Lincoln continued to campaign, delivering speeches in Chicago and other communities. On November 7, he was elected to the Illinois House of Representatives for the fifth time, but he decided to press on and run for a seat in the U.S. Senate instead.

Unfortunately, his bid for the Senate was unsuccessful. Nonetheless, Lincoln continued to speak out against the expansion of slavery, and his speeches from 1854 on attracted more favorable attention.

Certainly, Lincoln's political activities in 1854 were the beginning of a chain of events that led to his election to the presidency in 1860. As passage of the Kansas–Nebraska Act had influenced Lincoln in 1854, so would Lincoln have a profound effect on the course of history through his actions as president.

The speech that Lincoln delivered in Peoria in 1854 was a forceful statement against slavery. He insisted that the preservation of the nation depended on the spread of freedom, not bondage.

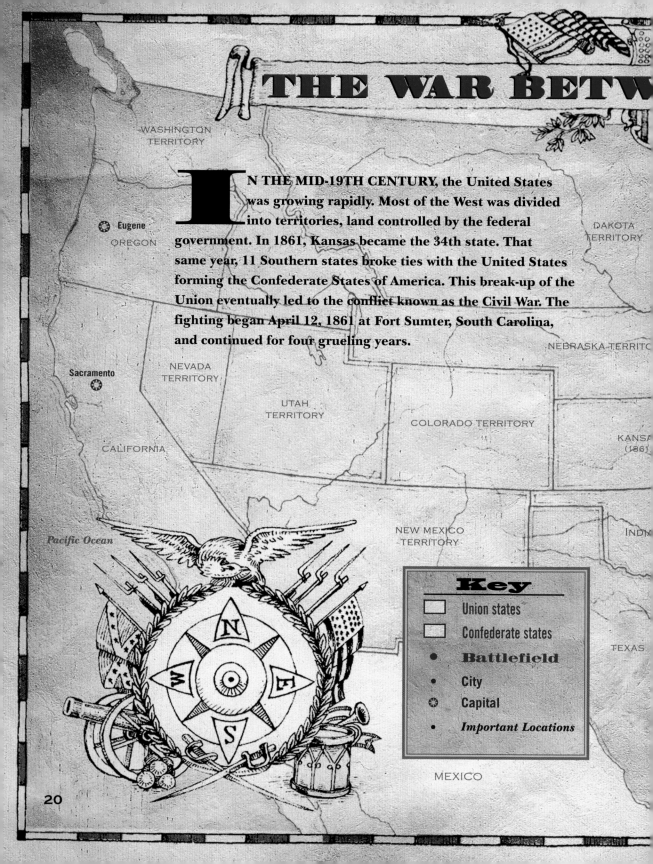

WASHINGTON
TERRITORY

Eugene
OREGON

DAKOTA
TERRITORY

IN THE MID-19TH CENTURY, the United States
was growing rapidly. Most of the West was divided
into territories, land controlled by the federal
government. In 1861, Kansas became the 34th state. That
same year, 11 Southern states broke ties with the United States
forming the Confederate States of America. This break-up of the
Union eventually led to the conflict known as the Civil War. The
fighting began April 12, 1861 at Fort Sumter, South Carolina,
and continued for four grueling years.

NEBRASKA TERRITO

Sacramento

NEVADA
TERRITORY

UTAH
TERRITORY

COLORADO TERRITORY

KANSA
(186)

CALIFORNIA

Pacific Ocean

NEW MEXICO
TERRITORY

INDI

Key

☐ Union states

☐ Confederate states

● **Battlefield**

• City

⊛ Capital

• *Important Locations*

TEXAS

MEXICO

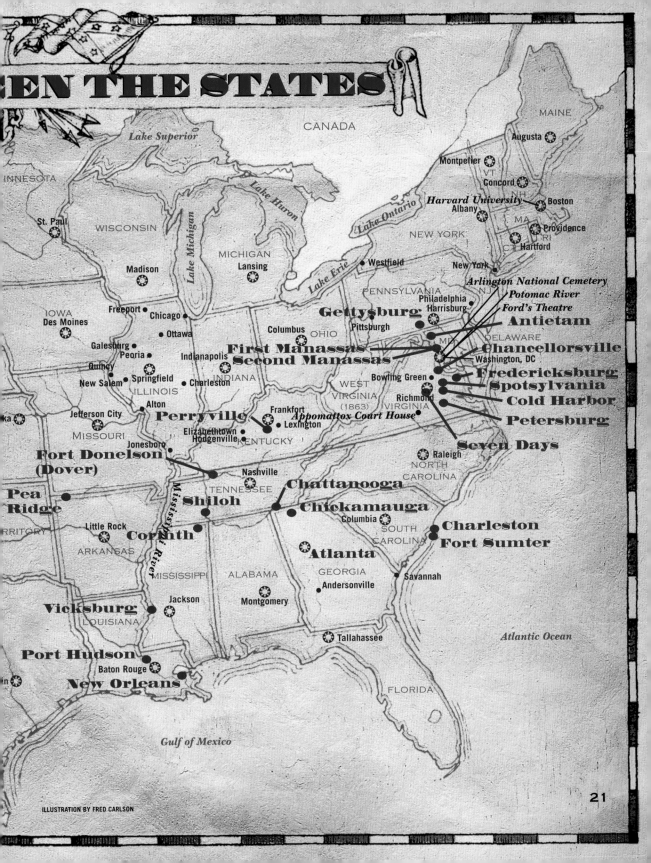

CANADA

MAINE

Lake Superior

Augusta ✱

Montpelier ✱

St. Paul ✱

MINNESOTA

Lake Huron

VT
Concord ✱
NH

Boston ✱

Harvard University

WISCONSIN

MICHIGAN

Lake Michigan

Albany ✱

MA

Providence ✱
RI
Hartford ✱
CT

Madison ✱

Lansing ✱

Lake Ontario

NEW YORK

New York ●

Lake Erie

Westfield ●

IOWA
Des Moines ✱

Freeport ●
Chicago ●

PENNSYLVANIA

Philadelphia ●
Harrisburg ●

Arlington National Cemetery

NJ

Potomac River

Gettysburg

Ford's Theatre

Columbus ●

Pittsburgh ●

Antietam

Ottawa ●

OHIO

Galesburg ●
Peoria ●

Indianapolis ●

DELAWARE

Chancellorsville

First Manassas
Second Manassas

MD

Quincy ●

New Salem ●

Charleston ●

INDIANA

Springfield ✱

WEST
VIRGINIA
(1863)

Bowling Green ●

— Washington, DC

Fredericksburg
Spotsylvania

ILLINOIS

Alton ●

Richmond ✱

VIRGINIA

Cold Harbor

Jefferson City ✱

Perryville

Frankfort ✱
● Lexington

Appomattox Court House

Petersburg

MISSOURI

ka ✱

Elizabethtown ●
Hodgenville ●

KENTUCKY

Seven Days

Jonesboro ●

Raleigh ✱

**Fort Donelson
(Dover)**

Nashville ●

Chattanooga

NORTH
CAROLINA

**Pea
Ridge** ●

Shiloh ●

TENNESSEE

Chickamauga ●

RRITORY

Little Rock ✱

Columbia ●

Corinth ●

Mississippi River

SOUTH
CAROLINA

Charleston

Fort Sumter

ARKANSAS

Atlanta ✱

GEORGIA

MISSISSIPPI

ALABAMA

Savannah ●

Vicksburg ✱

Jackson ✱

LOUISIANA

Andersonville ●

Montgomery ✱

Atlantic Ocean

Tallahassee ✱

Port Hudson

Baton Rouge ●

n ✱

New Orleans

FLORIDA

Gulf of Mexico

21

ILLUSTRATION BY FRED CARLSON

The Decision That Led to War

Four years before the Civil War began, the first shots were fired — not on a battlefield, but in the U.S. Supreme Court. This occurred in 1857, when the court considered a crucial question: Should a slave living in a free state be considered free?

Who Was Dred Scott?

Dred Scott was an African American slave owned by a man in Missouri. Scott then was sold to John Emerson, who took him to several states, including Illinois (a free state) and the Wisconsin Territory, which banned slavery under the Missouri Compromise. When Emerson died, his widow hired out Scott and his wife. The Scotts returned to Missouri, which allowed slaves to sue for their freedom.

Under Missouri law, once a slave was freed, that slave remained free forever. In 1846, Scott argued that he and his wife once were free because they had lived in Illinois

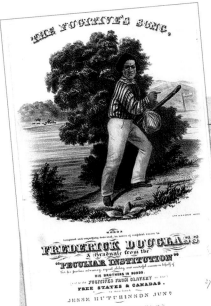

Escaping Slavery

In 1793, Congress passed the first Fugitive Slave Act to deal with runaway slaves. It allowed Southern slave owners to retrieve slaves who had escaped to Northern (free) states. Northerners responded by introducing "personal liberty laws" that would protect the fugitives. In 1850, the second Fugitive Slave Act required Northerners to assist in arresting runaway slaves and made it a crime to protect them.

and the Wisconsin Territory. A lower state court agreed. A higher court ruled that the Scotts still belonged to Mrs. Emerson.

In 1857 — 11 years after Scott instituted the suit — the case was decided by the Supreme Court in *Dred Scott v. Sandford*. The Court ruled that Congress did not have the power to prohibit slavery in the territories. More important for Scott, it also ruled that, when the Constitution was adopted, it granted citizenship to "every class and description of persons...recognized as citizens...." That "class" did not include "descendants of Africans who were imported into this country and sold as slaves...."

So, Scott was told that he had no right to sue in federal court — case dismissed.

Dred Scott, a slave who had traveled to free states with his master, claimed he was free. The Supreme Court denied his claim, and in the process overturned the Missouri Compromise, which enraged Northerners.

Shock Waves

The court's answer sent shock waves through every state, slave and free alike. According to the ruling, which became known as the Dred Scott decision, a slave would always be regarded as property, no matter where he or she happened to be.

Public reaction was swift and strong. Southerners expressed delight with the decision, claiming that it affirmed once and for all their right to keep slaves. Northerners expressed outrage, charging that the ruling was unjust and inhumane. In Illinois, future president Abraham Lincoln worried aloud that slavery would be permitted outside the South.

The Dred Scott decision set back the abolitionist cause and widened the gap between North and South concerning the explosive issue of slavery. The case aroused such passions that it helped bring on the Civil War, which ultimately signaled the end of slavery forever. Thus, although the Dred Scott decision ruled against one slave's hope for freedom, it helped bring about freedom for all slaves in the United States.

Abraham Lincoln and Stephen Douglas, candidates for the Illinois senate, debated their positions on slavery and states' rights. Large crowds attended each of the seven debates.

The Lincoln—Douglas Debates

In the mid-1800s, Ottawa, Illinois, was a small railroad town 70 miles southwest of Chicago. With a population of around 6,000, Ottawa led a rather quiet existence on the Illinois frontier. But at dawn on August 21, 1858, a great commotion stirred the sleepy town. From all directions, people converged on Ottawa. By train, by wagon, and on foot came such a multitude that soon a huge pall of dust rose over the town. From far and near, people had come to hear the first debate between Abraham Lincoln and Stephen Douglas.

The seven Lincoln–Douglas debates, held in various towns around the state, were arranged as part of the 1858 Illinois senatorial campaign. Douglas, the incumbent senator, was a powerful Democrat, thought by many to be a good choice for the presidency in 1860. He was a stocky man, about five feet tall, with a barrel chest and a head that was rather large in proportion to his body. Nicknamed "the Little Giant," Douglas had been a senator since 1847 and was chairman of the Senate Committee on Territories. In 1854, he authored the Kansas–Nebraska Act, a controversial bill that would help bring his long-time rival, Lincoln, back into the political arena.

Physically, Lincoln was about as different from Douglas as one could imagine. More than six feet tall, lean and rawboned, Lincoln was the favorite son of the newly formed Republican party. In contrast to Douglas, however, Lincoln's career as a lawyer and one-term member of the House of Representatives was singularly unremarkable. But the differences between the two men went deeper than appearance or career. On the ideological level, Lincoln and Douglas differed on the most important issue of the day: slavery.

Douglas felt that each state, particularly the new states, should decide whether or not to allow slavery. This was what Douglas called "popular sovereignty." It was obvious where Douglas stood on the issue of slavery: He did not feel it was wrong if the people wanted it.

Lincoln, who was personally against slavery, was not an abolitionist (one who insisted that slavery be outlawed totally). He did, however, oppose the spread of slavery. The young Republican party, itself against slavery, was looking for someone to oppose Douglas in the senatorial race. By a unanimous vote, the Republicans nominated Lincoln as their candidate. The stage was now set for the debates between "the Little Giant" and "the Rail-Splitter."

By noon, the sun shone brightly in the dusty sky over Ottawa. Brass bands played, cannon boomed, and flags flapped on the

Fast Fact

An estimated **78,400** spectators attended the 7 debates.

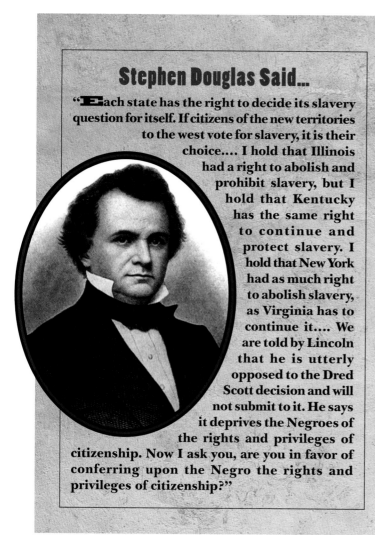

"Each state has the right to decide its slavery question for itself."

— Stephen Douglas

rooftops of stores and houses. About 12,000 people jammed the town square, eager to see and hear the two opponents. Reporters stood by to record every word with a new method of note taking called shorthand. For the first time, a political debate would be available to a mass audience through the newspapers.

At 2:30 P.M., everything was ready; the debate began.

Douglas, who spoke first, was an experienced orator. He accused Lincoln of being an abolitionist and of favoring a civil war. He explained his doctrine of popular sovereignty as the answer to the question of slavery in the United States. After an hour, it was Lincoln's turn. His sometimes shrill voice and informal manner were in distinct contrast to Douglas. Lincoln avoided specific replies to Douglas's accusations, preferring to think out his answers and respond at the next debate. He did, however, accuse Douglas of being part of a conspiracy to extend slavery into the territories, a charge that never was proved. Lincoln spoke for an hour and a half, then Douglas replied for 30 minutes more. After three hours of oratory, the debate ended, and each speaker's followers crowded

> "We think [slavery] is a moral, social, and political wrong."
>
> — Abraham Lincoln

around, cheering and applauding their candidate. This first debate had done little more than clarify the candidates' differing positions on slavery. Now it was on to Freeport and a debate that would spell trouble for Douglas.

Abraham Lincoln Said...

"We, the Republican Party, think slavery is wrong. We think it is a moral, social, and political wrong. We oppose it as an evil that seeks to spread across this country. We oppose the Dred Scott decision.... Mr. Douglas asks why the institution of slavery, or the Union part free and part slave, cannot continue as our fathers made it, forever. I insist that our fathers did not make this nation half slave and half free, or part slave and part free.... No reason has been furnished as to why the Negro is not entitled to all that the Declaration of Independence holds out, which is "life, liberty, and the pursuit of happiness.""

August 27 dawned chilly and damp in Freeport, but the weather could not dampen the enthusiasm of the almost 15,000 people who crowded into Goddard's Grove, the site of the second debate. This time Lincoln spoke first, responding to the accusations Douglas had made at Ottawa. Then Lincoln posed four questions to the Little Giant, one of which set a trap for Douglas. Lincoln asked Douglas to restate his endorsement of the Dred Scott decision, a Supreme Court ruling that made the outlawing of slavery in any territory unconstitutional. This seemed to conflict with the doctrine of popular sovereignty and put Douglas in a bind. Lincoln already

The Republican Party

Sometimes called the Grand Old Party, or GOP, the Republican party was created in 1854 by people who were opposed to the spread of slavery. The name *Republican* was chosen in remembrance of the Democratic-Republican party of Thomas Jefferson, also an opponent of slavery. The party's first presidential candidate, John C. Fremont, lost the 1856 election, but in 1860, Abraham Lincoln brought the Republican party to the White House.

knew how Douglas would answer; the point was to get him to say it for the reporters, and thus the entire nation, to hear.

The trap worked. It was true, Douglas said, that the Dred Scott decision made the spread of slavery legal. But, he added, the people of a territory could render this decision meaningless by not passing laws to protect slavery. Douglas's answer angered many southern Democrats, splitting the party and ultimately costing him the presidency in 1860.

Other debates took the candidates across the Illinois plains: Jonesboro, Charleston, Galesburg, Quincy, and finally Alton. By the end of the campaign, Lincoln and Douglas each had made approximately 60 speeches and had traveled thousands of miles by train, by wagon, and on foot. Now the only thing that remained was November 2, Election Day. When the votes were finally counted, Lincoln had 125,430 popular votes to Douglas's 121,609. But because the state legislature actually decided who would be senator and the legislative districts favored the Democrats, Douglas retained his Senate seat by a legislative vote of 54 to 46.

Disappointed that he had not become the U.S. senator from Illinois, Lincoln returned to his law practice in Springfield. Because of the national prominence he had gained through the debates, however, Lincoln soon would go to Washington in a much greater capacity: as the 16th president of the United States.

Lincoln's Beard

In 1860 a clean-shaven Lincoln was running for president. Grace Bedell, an 11-year-old from Westfield, New York, admired him, but she worried that he was too homely to win the election. So, she wrote Lincoln a letter—with a delightful suggestion.

I hope you wont think me bold to write to such a great man as you are, but want you should be President of the United States very much. I have got 4 brother's and part of them will vote for you any way, and if you will let your whiskers grow I will try to get the rest of them to vote for you. You would look a great deal better for your face is so thin. All the ladies like whiskers and they would tease their husbands to vote for you and then you would be President.

Grace was thrilled to receive an immediate, hand-written reply. Lincoln asked, "As to the whiskers, having never worn any, do you not think people would call it a silly piece of affec[ta]tion if I were to begin it now?" Nevertheless, only a few weeks after he won the election, Lincoln began to grow a beard.

Lincoln stopped in Westfield, New York, on the way to Washington for his inauguration. Hundreds of well-wishers came out to greet him. They were astonished when Lincoln asked if he could speak to Grace. A boy pointed toward the back of the crowd, and Lincoln stepped down from the train and made his way to where Grace stood. Then, the future president bent over and gave her "several hearty kisses."

Grace may not have changed the face of history, but she certainly changed the face of someone who did.

Leader of a Divided Nation

Lincoln's presidency was a challenge from the start. In the four months between his election and his inauguration, 7 Southern states seceded from the nation. The Civil War broke out the following month, and 4 more states seceded.

When Abraham Lincoln left his home in Illinois to begin the long journey to his inauguration as president, he told his neighbors he faced a task "greater than that which rested upon Washington." It was one of the most accurate predictions he ever made. No U.S. president before or after faced a graver crisis or emerged with a greater reputation.

Lincoln took his oath of office on March 4, 1861, assuring Southerners they had "no quarrel" with him. But quarrel they did. Southern states had already seceded and formed the Confederate States of America, presenting the most severe challenge to national authority in the country's brief history. Then in April, when Confederate forces opened fire on Fort Sumter, South Carolina, Lincoln promptly called for volunteers to defend the Union. The Civil War had begun.

'A People's Contest'

In a special Independence Day message to Congress in 1861, Lincoln called the struggle ahead "a people's contest." He was determined to preserve majority rule, warning that if democracy was defeated in America, it would surely never rise again anywhere in the world.

Words alone did not win victories. Just weeks later, Union forces were crushed at the First Battle of Manassas. A despairing Lincoln realized that the struggle would be long, costly, and bloody, but he steadfastly rejected suggestions that he abandon the war and allow the South to leave the Union in peace.

Union impatience was understandable. The North boasted more men and better technology. The South claimed a brilliant corps of generals, including Robert E. Lee, whom Lincoln had tried to recruit to head the Union army. The Union lost again at the Second Battle of Manassas (August 1862) and the Battle of Fredericksburg (December 1862), and Union forces failed to capture the Confederate capital of Richmond after a long campaign in Virginia.

Pushing the Union Cause

In September 1862, Lee, fearing that Southern supplies would eventually run out, invaded Maryland. There Union forces finally triumphed at the Battle of Antietam, the bloodiest single day in the history of American warfare. Lincoln seized on the victory to issue the Emancipation Proclamation, which pressured Southerners to free their slaves or surrender. He clearly hoped it would change the course of the war by threatening Southern productivity at home — where slaves still worked on farms and plantations while white men fought in the Confederate army.

Lincoln defended his momentous decision by declaring, "We cannot escape history." Although emancipation certainly did change history, it did not immediately change the course of the war. In May 1863, Lee handed the Union one of its worst defeats at the Battle of Chancellorsville.

The Stars Stay!

As Southern states dropped out of the Union, President Abraham Lincoln refused to remove their stars from the flag. He maintained that none of the Southern states ever legally left the Union.

An Unpopular War

Meanwhile, many antiwar Northerners were demanding peace and openly urging disloyalty to the Union. Lincoln created more controversy by allowing military arrests of civilians and prolonged confinement of suspects awaiting trial. The government defended both as attempts to crack down on treason.

Lincoln also ordered a military draft — a highly unpopular, badly conceived system in which wealthy men could buy their way out of service. In July 1863, New York City erupted in riots triggered by the draft. Mobs lynched innocent blacks and even burned an orphanage for black children.

Earlier in July, the North won a major victory at the Battle of Gettysburg in Pennsylvania and captured Vicksburg, Mississippi, the same week. But as 1863 drew to a close, Lincoln probably ranked as the most unpopular president in U.S. history.

Words of Wisdom

That November, Lincoln did with words what he had been unable to do with bullets. In a two-minute speech at Gettysburg, he rallied the North to what he called a "new birth of freedom" for America, vowing that government "of the people, by the people, for the people" would not "perish from the earth." It remains the greatest presidential speech ever given.

Lincoln met with General George B. McClellan (center, facing Lincoln) and other Union officers at Antietam in 1862, the site of one of the war's fiercest battles.

Lincoln also assumed an increasingly active role as commander in chief. It took him years to find the right generals — he hired and fired them with shocking swiftness in 1861 and 1862 — but eventually he found reliable leaders such as Ulysses S. Grant and William T. Sherman.

Strategic Decisions

In 1864, Lincoln made two major decisions, the importance of which is often overlooked. First, he allowed the presidential election to proceed as scheduled — something unheard-of in countries torn by rebellion. In addition, Lincoln decided to run again for the presidency. No president since Andrew Jackson had been reelected to a second term.

The 1864 campaign was one of the ugliest in U.S. history. Lincoln was challenged by one of his former generals, George B. McClellan. McClellan's backers accused Lincoln of supporting intermarriage between blacks and whites, a ploy designed to panic voters.

Until the last few weeks of the campaign, Lincoln believed that he would lose the election. He even asked his own cabinet to sign, sight unseen, a pledge to cooperate with the next president. And he secretly plotted with black leader Frederick Douglass to spread news of emancipation in the South to encourage slaves to flee their masters before the next president could overturn the order.

A huge crowd turned out for Lincoln's second inauguration on March 4, 1865. Lincoln (in circle) was the first president to be photographed at his inauguration. Inset: An illustration from a New York newspaper shows Lincoln taking the oath of office.

33

Hard-Won Victories

Two months before Election Day, Union forces captured Atlanta, Georgia, turning the tide of the war. Lincoln went on to defeat McClellan, winning 55 percent of the popular vote and 212 of 233 electoral votes.

Lincoln's finest moment may have come at his second inauguration on March 4, 1865. He defended the sacrifice of lives that had been necessary to rid America of the evil of slavery and called for an era of "malice toward none" and "charity for all" to "bind up the nation's

The Emancipation Proclamation

Through the summer of 1862, Lincoln labored over the paper that would help change the course of the war. When it was approved by his cabinet, he waited for a Northern victory that would give the announcement more impact. On September 22, Lincoln delivered the now famous Emancipation Proclamation. The Proclamation stated that unless the Confederacy surrendered by January 1, 1863, "all slaves in states or districts in rebellion against the United States on January 1, 1863, will be thenceforth and forever free." If the Confederacy surrendered, slavery would not be abolished.

But the Confederacy did not surrender on the first day of 1863, and abolitionists and freed slaves celebrated the historic change in America. When the celebration was over, however, they realized that the proclamation had not ended all slavery. Slaves in states that had not seceded from the Union were not freed, nor were slaves in places already defeated by the Union army. Not until 1865, when the Thirteenth Amendment of the Constitution was passed, was slavery abolished throughout the United States.

Following the Emancipation Proclamation, thousands of free blacks rushed to join the Union troops. The renewed strength of the Union army and the loss of plantation workers crippled the South, although the war dragged on for another two years. Lincoln's Proclamation helped end an era in American history, although blacks' struggle for equal rights would continue for many years to come.

wounds" and create "lasting peace among ourselves."

Triumph and Tragedy

The war ended a month later, and Lincoln began working on plans to reconstruct the devastated Union. He even hinted publicly that he would extend the right to vote to those black Americans who had fought to preserve the Union.

One of those who heard Lincoln offer that hope was an actor named John Wilkes Booth. An embittered Confederate sympathizer, Booth, with the help of several other conspirators, fatally shot Lincoln at Ford's Theatre on Friday, April 14, 1865. Nine hours later, Lincoln died in a boarding house across the street.

A man may have died, but a legend was quickly born. Hated by many while he lived, Lincoln was now universally celebrated as a latter-day Moses who had led black Americans to freedom and a beloved martyr who had died at the moment of his greatest triumph. More than ever, he seemed to symbolize American opportunity, for as Lincoln had put it, if he could rise from log cabin to White House, "any man's son" could hope to do the same.

Key Players
Frederick Douglass

In 1841, three years after he escaped from slavery, Frederick Douglass was asked to speak about his experiences as a slave. Thus began his career as an abolitionist, lecturer, writer, and publisher of an anti-slavery newspaper. With the onset of the Civil War, Douglass saw that his dream of freedom for blacks might come true, and he traveled the lecture circuit calling for President Abraham Lincoln to grant slaves their freedom. After Lincoln issued the Emancipation Proclamation freeing the slaves in Confederate states, Douglass worked even harder for black enlistment in the Union army, so blacks could fight to ensure their freedom.

In 1865, the Thirteenth Amendment officially abolished all slavery, and Douglass, then 47, thought about buying a farm and settling down to a quiet life. It soon became clear, however, that his work was not done, as blacks continued to suffer inequalities and injustices. For the rest of his 77 years, Douglass wrote and lectured in support of black suffrage and equal rights and worked as a political leader and government official, remaining the foremost spokesman for American blacks.

'I Laugh, Because I Must Not Cry'

Abraham Lincoln often had a look of sadness on his face, but he enjoyed few things more than a good joke. A childhood friend once said that even as a young boy, Lincoln was "so funny he could make a cat laugh." Years later, a newspaper called Lincoln "Chief Joker of the Land." Humor was his way of coping with the stress of a nation at war with itself.

Because he was skinny and not very handsome, Lincoln liked to tell jokes about himself. One favorite was his reply to Stephen Douglas during a debate, after Douglas called him a two-faced liar. "If I had another face," Lincoln said to the audience, "I ask you would I be wearing this one?"

A humorous story Lincoln told was about his first meeting with Mary Todd at a grand ball. Bowing to her, he nervously said that he would like to dance with her "in the worst way." A footsore Mary Lincoln later told a friend, "He certainly did."

As president, Lincoln often used wit with people who annoyed him. When General George B. McClellan kept refusing to engage the enemy in battle, Lincoln sent him a letter saying, "If you don't intend to use the army, won't you lend it to me?"

Lincoln certainly did not take the war lightly. In fact, the president, who suffered through spells of depression, felt a keen sense of responsibility for the bloodshed. To remain an effective president, he used his humor. "I laugh, because I must not cry," he once said.

> "To ease another's heartache is to forget one's own."
>
> **— Abraham Lincoln**

All this reminds me of a most capital joke.

Progress for a Stronger Nation

Abraham Lincoln won his greatest fame for saving the Union during the Civil War and issuing the Emancipation Proclamation. But in four years in the White House, Lincoln dealt with many other issues, and his handling of them still benefits Americans today.

Land-Grant Schools

During Lincoln's administration, for example, the nation began the program that led to today's state college system. The Morrill Act of 1862 required that money raised by the sale of public lands granted to each state be used for agricultural education. These land-grant schools later formed the basis for many state university systems still in operation.

Homestead Act

Also in 1862, Congress passed, and Lincoln signed into law, the Homestead Act, which offered Americans up to 160 acres of free land. This law did much to encourage the settlement of the West.

Communications

Before Lincoln became president, the United States had only primitive communication and transportation systems. But during his term in office, the country introduced its first free mail delivery service and its first coast-to-coast telegraph operation. Meanwhile, enormous progress was made in linking the nation together by rail.

The fact that the United States could make such progress during a rebellion shows the strength not only of its president but also of the country itself.

An illustration from an 1865 newspaper depicts the dramatic exit John Wilkes Booth made from Ford's Theatre after he fatally shot President Lincoln.

Conspiracy and Assassination

For several months, actor John Wilkes Booth's band of conspirators had plotted to capture Abraham Lincoln and hold him hostage in exchange for Confederate prisoners held by the North. Several early attempts had failed, and with Lee's surrender on April 9, 1865, Booth became desperate. "Our cause being almost lost," he wrote in his diary, "something decisive and great must be done."

Desperate Man, Wicked Plan

His opportunity to act came on Friday, April 14. Booth, an acclaimed actor, was at Ford's Theatre when word arrived from the White House: President and Mrs. Lincoln would attend that night's performance of *Our American Cousin*. The president was fatalistic about security, saying that no security system could stop an assassin, and he traveled with little protection.

Calling together his coconspirators, Booth mapped out a plan. As Lincoln was assassinated at Ford's Theatre, Secretary of State William Seward and Vice President Andrew Johnson would be killed as well. With one bold stroke, they surmised, the North would collapse in chaos.

'Stop That Man!'

That night, Booth strolled into Ford's Theatre just after 10 o'clock. Tipping his hat to the doorman, he crossed the lobby and climbed the stairs to the mezzanine. Finding the area unattended (the guard had taken a seat in the audience), Booth approached the door that led to the private boxes. Slipping into the dimly lit corridor, he shut the door and barred it from the inside.

Booth saw Lincoln seated in a rocker, silhouetted against the glowing stage lights beyond. The actor's hand closed around the handle of his revolver as he boldly stepped into the box. Leveling the pistol behind the president's left

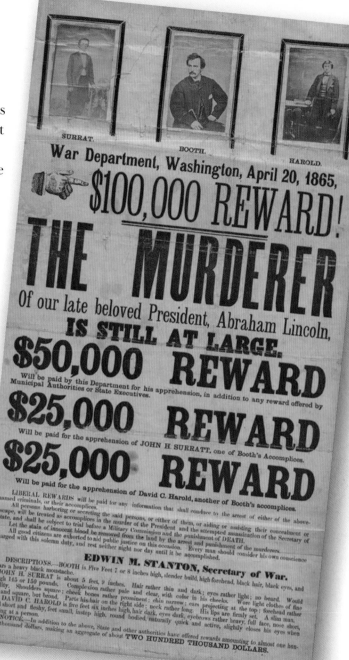

SURRAT.   BOOTH.   HAROLD.

War Department, Washington, April 20, 1865,

$100,000 REWARD!
THE MURDERER

Of our late beloved President, Abraham Lincoln,

IS STILL AT LARGE.

$50,000 REWARD
Will be paid by this Department for his apprehension, in addition to any reward offered by Municipal Authorities or State Executives.

$25,000 REWARD
Will be paid for the apprehension of JOHN H. SURRATT, one of Booth's Accomplices.

$25,000 REWARD
Will be paid for the apprehension of David C. Harold, another of Booth's accomplices.

LIBERAL REWARDS will be paid for any information that shall conduce to the arrest of either of the above-named criminals, or their accomplices.

All persons harboring or secreting the said persons, or either of them, or aiding or assisting their concealment or escape, will be treated as accomplices in the murder of the President and the attempted assassination of the Secretary of State, and shall be subject to trial before a Military Commission and the punishment of DEATH.

Let the stain of innocent blood be removed from the land by the arrest and punishment of the murderers.

All good citizens are exhorted to aid public justice on this occasion. Every man should consider his own conscience charged with this solemn duty, and rest neither night nor day until it be accomplished.

EDWIN M. STANTON, Secretary of War.

DESCRIPTIONS.—BOOTH is Five Feet 7 or 8 inches high, slender build, high forehead, black hair, black eyes, and wears a heavy black moustache.

JOHN H. SURRAT is about 5 feet, 9 inches. Hair rather thin and dark, with color in his cheeks; eyes rather light; no beard. Would weigh 145 or 150 pounds. Complexion rather pale and clear, with color in his cheeks. Wore light clothes of fine quality. Shoulders square; cheek bones rather prominent; chin narrow; ears projecting at the top; forehead rather low and square, but broad. Parts his hair on the right side; neck rather long. His lips are firmly set. A slim man.

DAVID C. HAROLD is five feet six inches high, hair dark, eyes dark, eyebrows rather heavy, full face, nose short, hand short and fleshy, feet small, instep high, round bodied, naturally quick and active, slightly closes his eyes when looking at a person.

NOTICE.—In addition to the above, State and other authorities have offered rewards amounting to almost one hundred thousand dollars, making an aggregate of about **TWO HUNDRED THOUSAND DOLLARS.**

Lincoln's murderer eluded capture for more than two weeks. This poster offers a reward for information leading to the arrest of John Wilkes Booth and his coconspirators.

ear, the assassin fired.

Confronted by Major Henry Rathbone, a guest in the presidential box, Booth dropped his gun, drew his dagger, and slashed the officer's arm to the bone. Booth quickly vaulted the railing, landing on the stage 12 feet below. As he jumped, his heel caught on a flag, and he landed awkwardly, breaking his left leg. Despite his pain, the actor got to his feet, held his dagger aloft, and cried, *"Sic semper tyrannis!"* ("Thus always to tyrants!") before fleeing to the rear of the theater.

Someone shouted, "Stop that man!" but pursuit was futile. Despite his injury, Booth had already mounted his waiting horse and escaped into the night.

John Wilkes Booth, above, planned Lincoln's murder for months. He enlisted the support of other Confederate sympathizers, from top to bottom, George Atzerodt, David Herold, Edward Spangler, Lewis Payne, and Mary Surratt.

The Death of Lincoln

The following morning, at 7:22 A.M., Lincoln died in a boarding house located across the street from the theater. A massive hunt for the assassin and his accomplices was launched. One of Booth's coconspirators, Lewis Payne (his real name was Lewis Thornton Powell), who had gone to Seward's house and brutally wounded the secretary of state, was arrested. George Atzerodt, who was sent to kill Johnson, also was caught, although he had lost his nerve and never attacked the vice president. Dozens more were taken into custody as Secretary of War Edwin Stanton vowed swift retribution for Lincoln's murderers.

Booth and David Herold, another coconspirator, eluded

capture. But when Booth's broken bone began "tearing the flesh at every jump," the two sought help at the Maryland home of Dr. Samuel Mudd. The doctor, who later denied any knowledge of the assassination, set Booth's leg and offered the travelers food and rest.

The Chase Ends

In the early hours of April 26, federal troops cornered Booth and Herold inside a tobacco shed in Bowling Green, Virginia. Herold was captured without a fight, but Booth refused to surrender and was shot. Just before he died, he whispered, "Tell Mother I died for my country."

Booth's coconspirators were tried by a military court without benefit of a jury. Payne, Atzerodt, and Herold were sentenced to "hang by the neck until dead." Another alleged coconspirator, Mary Surratt, also was hanged. The assassination plot had been hatched in her boarding house, although many still doubt her involvement.

Samuel Arnold and Michael O'Laughlin, who had deserted Booth long before the assassination, were sentenced to life in prison, as was Dr. Mudd. Edward Spangler, a stagehand at Ford's Theatre, was accused of helping Booth escape. He was sent to prison for six years.

The Nation Mourns

Lincoln's death came just five days after the Civil War ended. A time that should have been for celebration and mending was spent mourning the leader who had brought the nation through such turmoil.

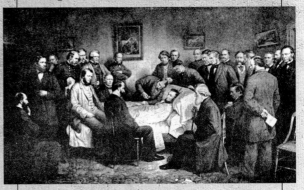

Four days after Lincoln's assassination, a funeral was held at the White House, followed by a procession through Washington. A unit of African American soldiers led the somber march. Lincoln's coffin was placed in the Rotunda of the Capitol, and thousands of people passed through to bid their president farewell.

A funeral train left Washington on April 21, carrying Lincoln's body back to his home in Springfield, Illinois, for burial. Along the way, mourners came out to watch with disbelief as the train passed. In Springfield, tens of thousands of people met the train and listened as bells tolled in the church and troops fired a salute.

Secretary of War Edwin M. Stanton said it best. He was at Lincoln's bedside when the president succumbed to his wounds. Stanton quietly stated, "Now he belongs to the ages."

Miss Ream's Statue

At the west entrance of the Rotunda stands a life-size statue of President Abraham Lincoln, lost in thought. The sculptor, Vinnie Ream, was only 17 years old when she created it.

Vinnie's friend, Representative James Rollins of Missouri, had asked Lincoln's permission for her to first make some drawings of the president. It was 1864, and Lincoln was worried about the latest battles of the Civil War. He ignored the request until he learned that Vinnie didn't have much money. "So she's young and poor, is she," he said. "Well, that's nothing agin' her. You may tell her she can come."

Over the last five months of the president's life, Vinnie watched him go about his duties and drew many sketches of him. Then, working in the basement of the Capitol, she carved her beautiful statue in plaster. Later, a carver re-created it in marble.

Vinnie was the first woman and the youngest artist ever to receive an assignment from the U.S. government. She also designed the first statue of a Native American — Sequoyah, inventor of the Cherokee alphabet — for the Capitol's National Statuary Hall. She is buried in Arlington National Cemetery in Virginia.

Vinnie Ream at work on her Lincoln bust, which rests upon the stand she used in the White House while President Lincoln posed for her.

A Poem for a President

President Abraham Lincoln's assassination immediately following the Civil War greatly affected poet Walt Whitman. He felt that Lincoln was a great hero and personified democracy.

Whitman wrote four poems honoring Lincoln. In "O Captain! My Captain!" Whitman imagines Lincoln as the captain of a ship. The captain has brought his vessel safely home (just as Lincoln had brought his nation through the war).

O Captain! My Captain!
by Walt Whitman

O Captain! my captain! our fearful trip is done;
The ship has weather'd every rack, the prize we sought is won;
The port is near, the bells I hear, the people all exulting,
While follow eyes the steady keel, the vessel grim and daring:
   But O heart! heart! heart!
   Leave you not the little spot,
   Where on the deck my captain lies,
   Fallen cold and dead.

Whitman

O Captain! my captain! rise up and hear the bells;
Rise up — for you the flag is flung — for you the bugle trills;
For you bouquets and ribbon'd wreaths — for you the shores a-crowding;
For you they call, the swaying mass, their eager faces turning;
   O Captain! dear father!
   This arm I push beneath you;
   It is some dream that on the deck,
   You've fallen cold and dead.

My captain does not answer, his lips are pale and still;
My father does not feel my arm, he has no pulse nor will;
But the ship, the ship is anchor'd safe, its voyage closed and done;
From fearful trip, the victor ship, comes in with object won:
   Exult, O shores, and ring, O bells!
   But I, with silent tread,
   Walk the spot my captain lies,
   Fallen cold and dead.

CIVIL WAR

1860

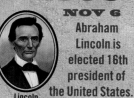
Lincoln

NOV 6
Abraham Lincoln is elected 16th president of the United States.

1861

FEB 9
Formation of the Confederate States of America (CSA) by secessionist states South Carolina, Mississippi, Florida, Alabama, Georgia, Louisiana, and Texas. Jefferson Davis elected CSA president.

Davis

MAR 4
Lincoln's inauguration

APR 12

Fort Sumter (South Carolina) Civil War begins with Confederate attack under Gen. Pierre Beauregard.

APR 15
Lincoln issues proclamation calling

---

for 75,000 troops. Gen. Winfield Scott becomes commander of Union army.

APR 17
Virginia joins CSA, followed by Arkansas, Tennessee, and North Carolina.

APR 20
Gen. Robert E. Lee resigns from U.S. Army and accepts command in Confederate army.

JUL 21
First Manassas (Virginia) Gen. Thomas J. "Stonewall" Jackson defeats Gen. Irvin McDowell.

NOV 1
Gen. George B. McClellan assumes command of Union forces.

1862

FEB 11-16
Fort Donelson (Tennessee) Gen. Ulysses S. Grant breaks major Confederate stronghold.

MAR
McClellan begins Peninsular Campaign, heading to Richmond,

Virginia, the Confederate capital.

APR 6-7
Shiloh (Tennessee) Grant defeats Beauregard and Gen. A.S. Johnston. Heavy losses on both sides.

APR 24

New Orleans (Louisiana) Gen. David Farragut leads 17 Union gunboats up Mississippi River and takes New Orleans, the South's most important seaport.

JUN 25-JUL 1
Seven Days (Virginia) Six major battles are fought over seven days near Richmond, Virginia. Lee is victorious, protecting the Confederate capital from Union occupation.

Halleck

JUL 18
Lincoln turns over command to Gen. Henry W. Halleck.

AUG 29-30
Second Manassas (Virginia) Jackson and Gen. James Longstreet defeat Gen. John Pope.

SEP 17
Antietam (Maryland) McClellan narrowly defeats Lee. Bloodiest day in American military history: 23,000 casualties.

SEP 22

Lincoln issues preliminary Emancipation Proclamation, freeing slaves in Confederate states.

OCT 3-4
Corinth (Mississippi) Gen. William Rosecrans defeats Gen. Earl Van Dorn.

NOTE: Battles are in black type, with flags indicating: Union victory 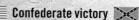 Confederate victory

TIME LINE

NOV 7
Lincoln replaces McClellan with Gen. Ambrose Burnside to lead Army of the Potomac.

Burnside

DEC 13
Fredericksburg (Virginia) Lee defeats Burnside.

1863

JAN 1
Final Emancipation Proclamation frees slaves in Confederate states. Union army begins enlisting black soldiers.

JAN 25
Lincoln replaces Burnside with Gen. Joseph Hooker.

Hooker

JAN 29
Grant is placed in command of the Union army in the West.

MAY 1-4
Chancellorsville (Virginia) Lee defeats Hooker.

JUN 28
Lincoln replaces Hooker with Gen. George E. Meade.

JUL 1-3

Gettysburg (Pennsylvania) Meade defeats Lee.

JUL 4
Vicksburg (Mississippi) After weeks of seige, Grant takes the Confederate stronghold on Mississippi River, effectively dividing eastern and western Confederate forces.

SEP 18-20
Chickamauga (Georgia) Gen. Braxton Bragg defeats Rosecrans.

OCT 16
Lincoln puts Grant in charge of all western operations.

NOV 19
Lincoln delivers the Gettysburg Address, dedicating the battlefield as a national cemetery.

NOV 23-25
Chattanooga (Tennessee) Grant defeats Bragg.

1864

MAR 9
Lincoln puts Grant in command of entire Union army. Gen. William T. Sherman takes over western operations.

MAY 8-21
Spotsylvania (Virginia) Grant defeats Lee.

MAY 31-JUN 12
Cold Harbor (Virginia) Lee defeats Grant and Meade.

JUN 15-18

Petersburg (Virginia) Lee and Beauregard defeat Grant and Meade.

NOV 8
Lincoln is re-elected.

NOV 15-DEC 21

Sherman's "March to the Sea." Sherman destroys supplies and transportation systems from Atlanta to Savannah (Georgia), crippling the Confederacy.

1865

Lee

APR 2
Petersburg (Virginia) Grant defeats Lee. Confederates leave Richmond.

APR 9
Lee surrenders to Grant at Appomattox Court House, Virginia.

APR 14
Lincoln is shot by John Wilkes Booth at Ford's Theatre, Washington, D.C. He dies the following morning.

DEC 6
Thirteenth Amendment to the Constitution abolishing slavery is ratified.

Glossary

Abolish: To get rid of completely. An *abolitionist* works to end slavery.

Accomplice: A person who helps carry out a crime.

Affectation: A style or behavior that is unnatural and showy.

Assassinate: To murder an important person, usually for political reasons. A person who commits an assassination is called an *assassin*.

Civil war: A war fought between people of the same nation.

Compromise: An agreement that ends conflict by requiring both sides to give in a bit.

Confederacy: In the American Civil War, the alliance of states that broke ties with the U.S. government to form a new government, called the Confederate States of America. The states that did not secede supported the Union.

Conspiracy: An organized plan to do something wrong or illegal. *Coconspirators* are people who work together to do something wrong.

Doctrine: A rule or set of laws that are the basic beliefs of a person, organization, or government.

Effigy: A dummy representing an enemy that is used as an object of abuse.

Emancipation: Freedom from slavery or other form of bondage.

Endorsement: An official show of support.

Enlist: Sign up for service in the military.

Fatality: An accidental death. Also, an event controlled by fate, destiny. A *fatalistic* person believes that fate controls future events.

Galvanize: To stir up action or support for a cause.

Ideological: Concerning the set of beliefs or issues held by an individual or group.

Immoral: Describes an act, behavior, or thought that is deemed bad. *Immorality* exists when people are immoral.

Inauguration: The formal beginning of a term in office.

Incumbent: The person who currently holds an elected office.

Inhumane: Lacking pity or compassion.

Legislature: A group of elected representatives whose job it is to make laws that govern a state or nation.

Lynch: To punish, often kill, someone without legal authority.

Mezzanine: In a theater, the lowest balcony.

Milk-sick: An illness caused by drinking the milk of cows that have eaten poisonous plants.

Orator: A skilled public speaker. *Oratory* refers to speeches.

Plantation: A large estate, often with resident workers, that produces income crops.

Repeal: To reverse an official act or law.

Secede: To make a formal withdrawal from an organization, alliance, or, in American history, a nation. Secession occurred when 11 states officially withdrew from the United States of America and formed a new nation, the Confederate States of America.

Sovereignty: Independence and self-government.

Sympathizer: To share the opinions and goals of a group, organization, or party.

Treason: A deliberate action that betrays one's country, such as aiding its enemies.

Unconstitutional: Something that goes against a nation's constitution (the basic set of laws that define a government and guide its decisions and direction).

Index

COBBLESTONE®
The CIVIL WAR Series

Few events in our nation's history have been as dramatic as those leading up to and during the Civil War. People held strong views on each side of the Mason-Dixon line, and the clash of North and South had far-reaching consequences for our country that are still being felt today.

Each 48-page book delivers the solidly researched content *COBBLESTONE®* is known for, written in an engaging manner that is sure to retain the attention of young readers. Perfect for report research or pursuing an emerging interest in the Civil War, these resources will complete your collection of materials on this important topic.

Each sturdy, hardcover volume includes:

- ■ Fair and balanced depictions of people and events
- ■ Well-researched text ■ Historical photographs
- ■ Glossary ■ Time line

$17⁹⁵ each

NATION AT WAR: SOLDIERS, SAINTS, AND SPIES	COB67900
YOUNG HEROES OF THE NORTH AND SOUTH	COB67901
ABRAHAM LINCOLN: DEFENDER OF THE UNION	COB67902
GETTYSBURG: BOLD BATTLE IN THE NORTH	COB67903
ANTIETAM: DAY OF COURAGE AND SACRIFICE	COB67904
ROBERT E. LEE: DUTY AND HONOR	COB67905
ULYSSES S. GRANT: CONFIDENT LEADER AND HERO	COB67906
STONEWALL JACKSON: SPIRIT OF THE SOUTH	COB67907
JEFFERSON DAVIS AND THE CONFEDERACY	COB67908
REBUILDING A NATION: PICKING UP THE PIECES	COB67909

Buy 3 books and get our Time Line Poster FREE!